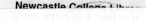

Homes
Around the World

Activity Book

Name: _____

Age: _____

Class: _____

School: _____

OXFORD
UNIVERSITY PRESS

OXFORD
UNIVERSITY PRESS

Great Clarendon Street, Oxford OX2 6DP

Oxford University Press is a department of the University of Oxford.
It furthers the University's objective of excellence in research, scholarship,
and education by publishing worldwide in

Oxford New York

Auckland Cape Town Dar es Salaam Hong Kong Karachi
Kuala Lumpur Madrid Melbourne Mexico City Nairobi
New Delhi Shanghai Taipei Toronto

With offices in

Argentina Austria Brazil Chile Czech Republic France Greece
Guatemala Hungary Italy Japan Poland Portugal Singapore
South Korea Switzerland Thailand Turkey Ukraine Vietnam

OXFORD and OXFORD ENGLISH are registered trade marks of
Oxford University Press in the UK and in certain other countries

ISBN: 978 0 19 464507 2

Printed in China

This book is printed on paper from certified and well-managed sources.

ACKNOWLEDGEMENTS

Homes Around the World Activity Book by: **Sarah Medina**

Illustrations by: Roger at KJA Artists, Alan Rowe, Martin Sanders/Beehive,
and Gary Swift

Introduction ← Page 3

1 Circle the correct words.

1 The earliest homes were **apartments** / (**caves**) / **bungalows**.

2 The **Incas** / **Romans** / **Greeks** in Peru built houses with stone blocks.

3 Nomads often live in **cottages** / **houseboats** / **tents** that can be folded up and carried.

4 The Inuit people in **the Arctic** / **Thailand** / **Mongolia** build winter homes with snow.

5 There's no electricity or running water in **cities** / **apartments** / **shanty towns**.

6 North American wagons were pulled by **dogs** / **oxen** / **elephants**.

2 Answer the questions.

1 Where do you live?

_____

2 What types of home are there where you live?

_____

_____

3 What type of home do you live in?

_____

1 Homes in the Past ← Pages 4–7

1 Complete the sentences. Then number the pictures.

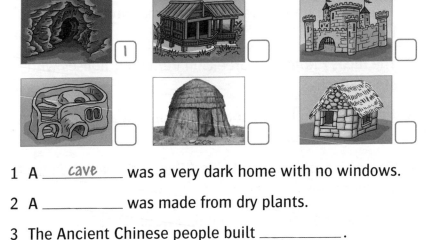

1 A _____cave_____ was a very dark home with no windows.

2 A _____ was made from dry plants.

3 The Ancient Chinese people built _____.

4 Some people built _____ because they were strong.

5 Important rich people built _____.

6 A _____ had a hole in the wall for a door.

2 Complete the chart.

~~dark~~   dry bricks   thatched roofs   bamboo roofs
cut blocks   flat roofs   platforms   animal skin doors

Caves	Straw and Mud Houses	Stone Houses	Wooden Houses
dark			

3 Number the people in order (1 = earliest). Then write how many years ago.

1 [5] Ancient Romans _2,000 years ago_

2 [ ] Incas _____

3 [ ] Ancient Egyptians _____

4 [ ] Ancient Greeks _____

5 [ ] Ancient Chinese _____

6 [ ] Cave people _____

4 Match. Then write complete sentences.

in caves

on Inca houses

in straw houses

in some Roman houses

in stone castles

on an Egyptian house

there was
there were

holes in the walls for windows

a flat roof

a bathroom

rich people

no kitchen or bathroom

thatched roofs

1 _In caves, there was no kitchen or bathroom._

2 _____

3 _____

4 _____

5 _____

6 _____

(2) Homes Today ← Pages 8–11

1 Write the words. Then complete the chart.

1 a p a rt m e n t

2 c _ _ cr _ _ e

3 g _ _ _ s

4 t _ rr _ _ e _ h _ _ se

5 w _ _ d

6 s _ _ _ e

7 b _ _ g _ _ o _

8 c _ _ t _ g _

9 m _ _ s _ _ n

10 p _ _ st _ _

Materials	Types of Home
	apartment

2 Circle and write the correct words.

1 Some poor families share one _____ .
   swimming pool / bathroom / mansion

2 A _____ has lots of very poor homes together.
   garden / shelter / shanty town

3 Homeless people sometimes sleep in _____ .
   cardboard boxes / apartments / bungalows

3 **Order the words. Then write *true* or *false*.**

1 people / small / sometimes / Poor / apartments. / share

Poor people sometimes share small apartments. _true_

2 made / homes / man-made / are / Many / materials. / with

_____ _____

3 apartments / in / skyscrapers. / are / Some / tall

_____ _____

4 them. / have / all / Terraced / space / around / houses

_____ _____

5 all / rooms / Bungalows / the / two / on / floors. / have

_____ _____

6 is / bricks / of / A / and / thatched / cottage / has / made / a / roof.

_____ _____

4 **Answer the questions.**

1 What is an apartment?

_____

2 Why do people often have gardens or land?

_____

3 What is teak very good for?

_____

4 Why can't poor people buy or build their own home?

_____

③ Different Climates 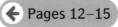 Pages 12–15

1 Write the climates.

1 ___polar___

2 _____

3 _____

4 _____

5 _____

2 Match the opposites. Then complete the sentences.

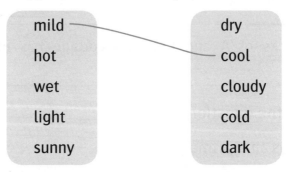

mild	dry
hot	cool
wet	cloudy
light	cold
sunny	dark

1 In temperate climates the weather is usually ___mild___.

2 In _____ mountainous climates homes are often built with stone.

3 In _____ deserts it is very hot in the day and cold at night.

4 In tropical climates the weather is _____.

5 Thick walls keep houses _____ in the day and _____ at night.

3 Order the words. Then write *true* or *false*.

1 temperate / the / In / weather / usually / climates / cold. / is

_____ _____

2 water / keep / and / in / homes / Bricks / wet. / keep

_____ _____

3 light / cold. / fire / when / People / can / a / is / it

_____ _____

4 have / eleven / ten / igloos / or / Some / rooms.

_____ _____

5 people / In / underground. / deserts / homes / make / some

_____ _____

4 Match. Then write complete sentences.

in tropical climates		quite warm inside
in temperate climates		often floods
in cold climates		usually cold
in Arctic igloos	there are	cool but dark
in desert houses with small windows	it is	often stone houses

1 _____

2 _____

3 _____

4 _____

5 _____

4 Homes that Move

Pages 16–19

1 Complete the sentences. Then number the pictures.

1 People who live in __________ can travel and take their home with them.

2 Some __________ are used as floating shops.

3 In North America __________ were pulled by oxen.

4 __________ are like big cars or vans that people can live in.

2 Complete the sentences.

1 Many people in Mongolia are n o m a d s.

2 Some Arctic Inuit tents are made from deer _ _ _ _ _ and whale _ _ _ _ _.

3 A floating house is made from _ _ _ _ _ _ _.

4 Many people like to drive in RVs on _ _ _ _ _ _ _ _ _ _.

5 When people go camping they cook outside on a _ _ _ _.

3 Order the words. Then answer the questions.

1 some / nomads / in / live? / do / Mongolia / Where

   Where do some nomads in Mongolia live?

   Some nomads live in gers.

2 floating / Who / in / makes / Peru? / houses

   _____

   _____

3 What / used / houseboats / some / as? / are

   _____

   _____

4 pulled / in / What / America / North / 150 / ago? / wagons / years

   _____

   _____

5 do / Where / sleep? / camping / go / who / people

   _____

   _____

4 Answer the questions.

1 What were teepees made from?

   _____

2 When people go camping, where do they sleep?

   _____

3 What are modern wagons called?

   _____

5 Famous Homes ← Pages 20–23

1 Write the famous homes.

1 $gh_unB^c_{i}m^ak\ l_ea^Pa_c$ <u>Buckingham Palace</u>

2 $e^hT\ _iw^eh_t\ o^Hs_ue$ _____

3 $^nw_io^rd_s\ s_te^Ca_l$ _____

4 $^hTe\ d^r_ofb^ie_nd\ i_c^yt$ _____

5 $p^aT_ip^ko\ cl_ae^aP$ _____

2 Complete the sentences.

> November   sultans   buildings   largest
> 1800   earthquakes   museum   ~~15~~   president   4,000

1 The Forbidden City took _____15_____ years to build.

2 The Forbidden Palace has nearly 1,000 _____.

3 Today the Forbidden City is a _____.

4 Windsor Castle is one of the _____ castles in the world.

5 It took 15 hours to put out the fire at Windsor Castle in _____ 1992.

6 The White House is the home of the American _____.

7 The first White House was built in _____.

8 Topkapi Palace in Turkey was home to the _____.

9 Up to _____ people lived in Topkapi Palace.

10 Some parts of Topkapi Palace were destroyed by fires and _____.

3 Answer the questions.

1 How many rooms does the White House have?

_____

2 How many people worked in the kitchens of Topkapi Palace?

_____

3 What is the largest ancient palace in the world?

_____

4 How many presidents have lived in the White House?

_____

5 Where is the Forbidden City?

_____

6 Who is buried at Windsor Castle?

_____

4 Write about your home. Use some of these words.

room   door   window   ~~floor~~   bathroom   garden   elevator

1 My home has _____ floors.

2 _____

3 _____

4 _____

5 _____

6 _____

6 Unusual Homes ← Pages 24–27

1 Write the words. Then answer *yes* or *no*.

		Can you build with it?
1 trcOneeC	concrete	yes
2 cyleceiritt	_____	_____
3 obta	_____	_____
4 skricb	_____	_____
5 veac	_____	_____
6 noset	_____	_____
7 dowo	_____	_____
8 nowdiw	_____	_____
9 dmu	_____	_____
10 nicehym	_____	_____

2 Order the words. Then write *true* or *false*.

1 People / Guadix / in / don't / caves. / sleep / in

_____   _____

2 usually / no / Cave / have / and / water / homes / electricity.

_____   _____

3 people / their / Some / different. / want / look / house / to

_____   _____

4 Homes / built / an / shape. / are / never / in / unusual

_____   _____

5 sometimes / things / nature. / from / Architects / copy

_____   _____

3 Match. Then write complete sentences.

many caves	houses with boat-shaped roofs
one house in New Mexico	a house made from plastic bottles
a diamond-shaped house in Japan	televisions and Internet connections
in Indonesia, some people	four walls and a roof
a woman in El Salvador	walls made of mud, tires, and cans
most homes around the world	a parking space for the car

have
has

1 _____

2 _____

3 _____

4 _____

5 _____

6 _____

4 Answer the questions.

1 How many people in Guadix live in cave homes?

_____

2 In underground caves, what are chimneys for?

_____

3 How long did it take the woman in El Salvador to build her house?

_____

7 Homes for Everyone 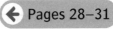 Pages 28–31

1 Write the words. Then answer the question.

1 $r_ir_uce_nh_a$ _____

2 $kaq_ae_hu_rt_e$ _____

3 d_lof_o _____

4 a_rw _____

Where do people live when their homes are destroyed by these things?

In _ _ _ _ _ _ _ _ _ _ _ _ _.

2 Complete the sentences. Use the words in the box.

> orphanage   poles   door   *yano*   roof   ladders
> windows   rooms   floors   *tulou*   hammocks   leaves

1 In Mexico, people sometimes use _____ to get

between _____. In summer they may sleep on the

_____ because it is cool there.

2 In China, a big round house made of mud is called a

_____. In a *tulou*, all the main _____ are inside.

There is only one _____ in a *tulou*. Each family in a

tulou has two or three _____.

3 The Yanomami people live in a big round home called a

_____. In a *yano*, people sleep in _____. A *yano*

is built with wooden _____ and has a thatched roof

made from _____.

4 Children with no parents sometimes live in an _____.

3 **Order the words. Then write *true* or *false*.**

1 families / live / same / Sometimes / in / lots / building. / of / the

_____   _____

2 together. / parts / In / the / live / different / of / world / many / generations

_____   _____

3 *tulou* / a / round / made / wood. / house / big / is / of

_____   _____

4 America / live / built / In / most / for / in / families. / people / North / homes / two

_____   _____

4 **Match. Then write complete sentences.**

lots of people		in the Amazon rainforest
in each village, everybody		near his or her family
the Yanomami people	live	together in a *tulou*
when many homes are destroyed, people	lives	in refugee camps all over the world
sometimes an old person		together in refugee camps
about 12 million people		together in a *yano*

1 _____

2 _____

3 _____

4 _____

5 _____

6 _____

8 Future Homes Pages 32–35

1 Write the words. Then complete the chart.

1 s _ r _ w   4 s _ _   7 _ _ l

2 gr _ s _   5 f _ _ m   8 g _ _

3 _ o _ l   6 c _ m _ _ t   9 _ in _

Environmentally Friendly	Not Environmentally Friendly

2 Write about your home and your future home.

In my home, I have _____

_____

_____

In my future home, I will have _____

_____

_____

_____

18

3 Complete the sentences.

1 Energy from coal, oil, and gas is bad for the _____ .

Homes in the future will be more _____ . They will use

clean energy from the _____ and the _____ .

2 It is good to save _____ in our homes. Homes that are

_____ stop energy escaping through roofs, doors, and

_____ .

4 Order the words. Then write *true* or *false*.

1 with / walls / fall / Homes / hurricane. / in / steel and concrete /
will / down / a

_____ _____

2 from / environmentally / the / friendly. / sun / is / Energy

_____ _____

3 friendly. / house / inside / with / is / straw / A /
environmentally

_____ _____

4 Our / not / are / changing. / climates

_____ _____

5 designing / that / Architects / homes / float. / will / are

_____ _____

6 cement and foam / New / are / made / homes / heavy. / from

_____ _____

After Reading 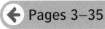 ← Pages 3–35

1 Check your answers to Activity 1, page 3.

1 = caves   2 = Incas   3 = tents   4 = the Arctic
5 = shanty towns   6 = oxen

2 Complete the puzzle.

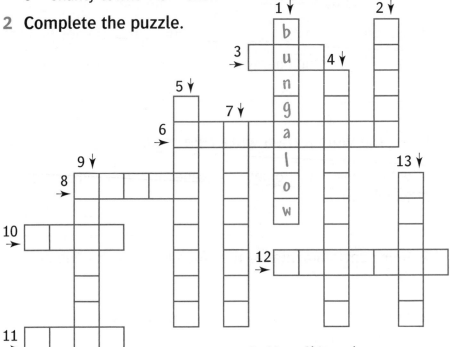

7 Many Chinese houses were built on a __.

1 A __ has all the rooms on one floor.

2 __ houses are very strong.

3 The Ancient Egyptians built houses with bricks made of __ and straw.

4 In big cities many people live in __.

5 A __ can be used as a floating shop.

6 Some children with no parents live in an __.

8 About 50,000 years ago people lived in __.

9 A __ is usually pulled by a car.

10 Nomads in Mongolia live in tents called __.

11 Yanomami people live together in a __.

12 Rich people sometimes live in a __.

13 Inuit homes made from snow are called __.

3 Write the words. Then find and write the page.

1 These homes were dark and did not
have windows. ___caves___ ___page 4___

2 This is the main home of the Queen of the
United Kingdom. _____ _____

3 This house made with stone and wood is built
in cold mountainous climates. _____ _____

4 This is where old people sometimes
live together. _____ _____

5 This is another word for a ranch
house. _____ _____

6 In tropical climates some people build
homes on these. _____ _____

7 These people built houses with bricks made
of mud and straw. _____ _____

8 In these homes people will use one computer
for everything. _____ _____

9 These nomad tents can be folded
up and carried. _____ _____

10 These homes are used as floating homes, and
sometimes as floating shops. _____ _____

11 This is where the president of the
USA lives. _____ _____

12 These homes often have expensive furniture,
big gardens, and swimming pools. _____ _____

4 Match. Then complete the chart.

live   build   take   sleep   protect   travel   share   keep

built   slept   traveled   kept   took   protected   lived   shared

Regular Verbs	Regular Past Tense	Irregular Verbs	Irregular Past Tense
live	lived		

5 Complete the sentences.

1 About 5,000 years ago people _____lived_____ in caves. (live)

2 In cities today many people _____ in apartments. (live)

3 Caves _____ people from wild animals. (protect)

4 Some poor families now _____ one home. (share)

5 Ancient Egyptians often _____ on the roof because it was cool. (sleep)

6 Some nomads live in gers and _____ around with their animals. (travel)

7 In an old people's home people _____ each other company. (keep)

6 Complete the chart with ✓ or X. Then write two sentences about each type of home.

		Round	Two or More Floors	Mud	Windows	Thatched Roof	Bricks or Stone	Wood
1	*Yano*	✓						
2	Mansion							
3	*Tulou*							
4	Cottage							

1 A yano is round.

2

3

4

My Book Review

Homes
Around the World

Title of this book: _____

Name of the author: _____

This book is about different types of _____.

Questions about this book

1 What new words did you learn from this book? (Write six words.)

_____

_____

2 What was the most interesting home in the book? Why?

_____

_____

3 What is your favorite type of home? Why?

_____

_____

What I like about this book

My favorite chapter was _____.

My favorite picture was _____.

My scores for this book (draw ☺, ☺☺, or ☺☺☺)

Interesting book ◯◯◯   Interesting cover ◯◯◯

Interesting pictures ◯◯◯   Fun to read ◯◯◯

Which book do you want to read next? _____